S0-ATL-226

ZOMBIE
THE LIVING DEAD

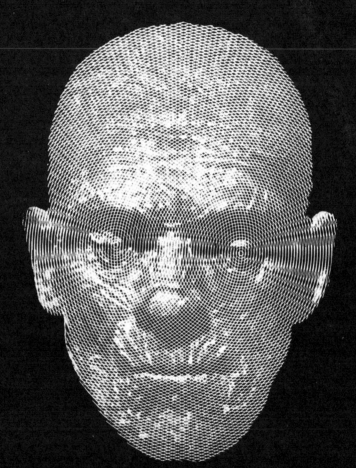

"It couldn't be done"—
So Universal did it!

The Mummy
(A KARLOFF Classic)

ZOMBIE
THE LIVING DEAD

ROSE LONDON

BOUNTY BOOKS
NEW YORK

Copyright © MCMLXXVI by Lorrimer Publishing Ltd
Library of Congress Catalog Card Number: 76-25725
All rights reserved.
This edition is published by Bounty Books
a division of Crown Publishers, Inc.
by arrangement with Lorrimer Publishing Ltd,
47 Dean Street, London W1.

Printed in the U.K. by
W. & J. Mackay Ltd., Chatham

Designers: Dave Allen and Graham Bingham

Cover design by Robert Ellis

CONTENTS

We wish to give our thanks in the preparation of this book to RKO, 20th Century Fox, Paramount, MGM, Columbia-Warner and Joy Smith, United Artists, Allied Artists, First National, Universal, EMI and Mike Buist and John Fraser Fox-Rank and Barbara de Law, British Lion, Davidson-Dallings, Hammer Films, Cinema International Corporation and Denis Michael, the British Film Institute stills department, the Cinema Bookshop, the Museum of Modern Art, Al Reuter, Brian McIlmail, Martin Jones, Walt Lee, Jerry Fiore and many others.

THE FEAR OF THE UNDEAD

We have always wanted to live for ever. The greater we are, the heavier the piles of stone which we put over our bones. These vaults and tombs are meant to show how magnificent our lives were — or to prevent our corpses from getting up again from under all that weight. As the architect Vanburgh's epitaph went : 'Lie heavy on him, Earth, for he has laid many a heavy weight on you'.

The Pharaohs of Egypt set the fashion for the cult of the honoured dead with their vast pyramids. Hidden in the middle of these stone labyrinths in a sealed chamber under the lid of a sarcophagus, they were embalmed and wrapped in bandages to resist corruption and decay in

Karloff as the embalmed High Priest in Karl Freund's *The Mummy* (1932).

their airless confinement. The discovery of these bandaged monarchs of ancient times led to a whole genre of movies of the undead, which relied on the publicity given to the finding of Tutunkhamen's tomb and other royal treasures. It was fortunate that the first of the Mummy pictures featured the great Boris Karloff himself. If he did not reproduce his classic waking sequence of *Frankenstein* in the scene in which the mummy comes alive, he did depict one superb moment of terror in a flashback sequence to ancient Egypt. Then he played the High Priest Im-Ho-Tep as he was embalmed alive for stealing the magic Scroll of Thoth, in order to revive his dead love. As the tape was drawn across his mouth and nose, Karloff's wild eyes staring at the prospect of eternal sleep are an instant of screen genius.

The relative success of *The Mummy* in 1932 led to many walkabouts by actors and actresses revived from the dead and unwrapped from their bandages. They fell into two categories. There were the terrifying cloth-bound creatures, who seemed to have wandered out of a ter-minal casualty ward. Footage from Karloff's *The Mummy* was actually used in two of these remakes, *The Mummy's Hand* of 1940 and *The Mummy's Curse* of 1945. In that second sequel, Lon Chaney Jr. played Kharis the Mummy, looking blurred and groping for the scared girl in white.

The mummy became such a figure of mass fantasy in the other remakes of the 1940s such as *The Mummy's Tomb* and *The Mummy's Ghost* that both The Three Stooges and Abbott and Costello decided to meet the mummy.

So the corpses of the Pharaohs became a laugh, and the shrieks turned into a giggle. And as with the Dracula pictures, what Universal unwrapped, Hammer Films wrapped up. Christopher Lee played *The Mummy* for Hammer in 1959, and Eddie Powell played it again in 1966 in *The Mummy's Shroud.* In the second of these unscaring pictures, we were told by the poster: 'Beware the beat of the cloth-wrapped feet!' In fact, it was only the sound of the audiences not coming to the cinema.

Another variant on the theme of the

Abbott and Costello Meet the Mummy in 1955.

Above: Valerie Leon is wakened from the sleep of ages by the severed hand in *Blood from the Mummy's Tomb* (1971). *Below:* The mummies of Guanajuato seem to be coming back from the dead.

Above: The old lady advances, backed by the mummies of Guanajuato.
Below: The mummies of Guanajuato wait to attack the superheroes.

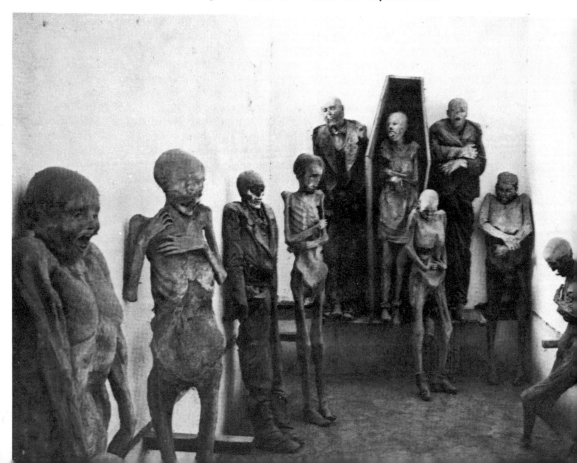

The undead mutants threaten the
lovers in Roger Corman's *The Haunted
Palace* (1963).

mummy was the resurrection of the
beautiful Egyptian princess or priestess,
who was revived in her unearthly beauty.
The Mummy's Curse had set the Sleeping
Beauty tradition of the awakening of the
lovely maiden, and it was carried to its
limits by the hilarious shocker, *Blood
from the Mummy's Tomb* of 1972. In that
mish-mash of Egyptiana with a probing
severed hand crawling about under the influence of a sacred jewel, the superb
Valerie Leon played the princess, revived
by this grope across the centuries into a
reincarnation routine.

Not all mummies were royal. The
people also died. Some of those buried
were dehydrated and petrified by natural
causes. The most famous of these are the
mummies of Guanajuato in Mexico. The
graveyard on the hillside there is small
and swept by winds and scoured by the
sun. Every few years, the dead are dug up
again to make room for more recent
corpses. One in ten of these older bodies
are found to have become natural mummies. They are preserved in vaults and
shown off to tourists. Unfortunately,
many seem to have died screaming — or
to be coming back to life again.

The Mexican cinema has not ignored
these home-grown mummies. Three
movies have been made about them
reviving to battle the local Mexican
superheroes, Santo and Superzan, Blue
Demon and Blue Angel, Mil Mascaras
and Tinieblas — the Man of the Thousand
Masks and Darkness. The mummies have
an eerie power as they keep rising from
the dead. They stand in wait as horribly
as a street gang of mutants, looking for
their victims.

The trouble with the undead rising in
legend is that they rise corrupt, their
bodies and faces dissolved or withered.
The Scots Ballads are full of stories of
mother's wishes being granted and dead
sons returning from drowning, green and
dripping, or from the graveyard in their
winding-sheets with the worms dropping
from them. Unfortunately, memory keeps
the young forever young in the mind, but
the tomb does not. It is one of the

Above: The vampire's young victim suddenly dies of old age as the blood is drained from her veins in *Captain Kronos — Vampire Hunter* (1972). *Below:* The young girl faints in front of the old crone in *The Hand of Night* (1966), when she sees what has escaped from the tomb.

Lon Chaney Jr. stands in his coffin, waiting to lurch out of it, in *Face of the Screaming Werewolf* (1965). In this mish-mash, Chaney played mummy, werewolf and zombie.

frequent shock tactics of the cinema to show the sudden aging of the beautiful girl, or to contrast the lovely with the hideous.

The fear of the return of the buried in their foul state of decomposition has been a staple of the horror cinema. Audiences shudder agreeably to see human clay not too perfectly formed by the make-up artist, as in *Cures of the Faceless Man. (See Colour Section)*. There is also a positive pleasure in making the undead rise from their graves, even unwillingly. Poor old Lon Chaney Jr. was always having to appear behind a putrid mask, slower and slower as he played the walking corpse over and over again.

The bodies of the dead, their skulls and skeletons, are the subjects of witchcraft, ritual and fear. A documentary such as *Tabu* with a commentary by Vincent Price is presented as a horror movie, and it shows where the ancient rites of primitive peoples enter the celluloid exploitation of ancient fears. In a cheap shocker such as *Death Curse of Tartu*, old Indian rituals are used in the plot of a Seminole witchdoctor returning from the grave and transferring his unquiet spirit into various animals. Lost in prehistory are our atavistic beliefs in the power of the undead to rise again and possess the shapes of animals, or to come avenging from the mists like the hanged man's ghost in the *Strangler of the Swamp*.

The power and the life of human skeletons is a very old belief. Witchdoctors in tribal countries still prophesy the future from shaking human bones together, predicting from the patterns in

Lon Chaney Jr. rises again from the tomb in *Dr. Terror's Gallery of Horrors* (1967).

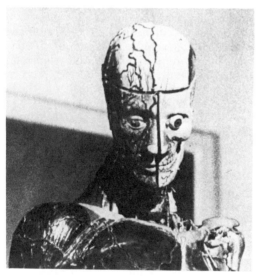

A mummy's head, ritually sliced open, from *Tabu* with its commentary spoken by the king of the macabre, Vincent Price.

The living skull of the Seminole witchdoctor from *Death Curse of Tartu* (1966).

which these bones fall. In the classical Greek legend of *Jason and the Argonauts*, the dragon's teeth were sown and emerged as armed and murderous skeletons.

In the Middle Ages, the skeletons of the dead were meant to rise again in the spring and lead women in a dance of death, commemorating the yearly ritual of birth and dying of the seasons. Even the first horror movie, a magic lantern show of 1800, presented an armed skeleton apparently attacking the audience. Ladies were so frightened that they fainted in the arms of their escorts, one of whom drew a sword and cut the screen to pieces. And crap-shooters still shout, 'Shake them bones!' to make the dice fall their way.

In the Hindu religion, indeed, death is alive. Kali, the goddess of death, has many arms to cut down the lives which are her due. There was even a cult of killers called the Thuggees, who murdered for her benefit and their own, sending on thousands of people before their time to act as Kali's servants in the next world. Or course, the Thuggees had the benefit of the goods Kali's servants left behind them.

The ghosts of the undead coming back to earth have not been well shown outside the Japanese cinema. Yet in the Japanese version of Macbeth, *Throne of Blood*, Banquo's unquiet ghost and the lone witch are marvels of hazy terror. And in that masterpiece of a trilogy of ghost stories, *Kwaidan*, the ghost lady is as beautiful and spectral as any stealer of the human soul should be. In *Kuroneko* also, the ghost girl comes back to avenge herself on men as a vampire and as a black cat — a dangerous bedfellow even for such a sensual night.

Of course, there were literal Resurrectionists, to give them their old name. They were otherwise known as *The Body Snatchers*, the name of a Karloff and Lugosi vehicle of 1945. They robbed graveyards for corpses to sell to the early surgeons and anatomists, and in the notorious case of Burke and Hare in Edinburgh, they also killed the living to add to their profits. Karloff turned in one of his

Jason fights to the death against the attacking skeletons.

The dance of death from *La Dance Macabre des Femmes,* Paris, 1486.

An early magic lantern show scares its audience.

Kali, the Indian goddess of death.

The beautiful ghost lady in *Kwaidan* (1963).

The Japanese Macbeth confronts the lone witch in Kurosawa's *Throne of Blood* (1957).

Above: The vampire cat girl in *Kuroneko* (1968). *Below:* Boris Karloff at his best in *The Body Snatcher* (1945).

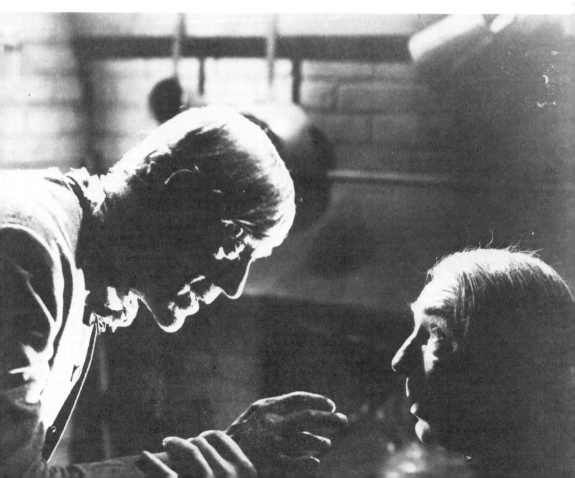

Christopher Lee as Count Drago in _Castle of the Living Dead_ (1964).

finest performances as the evil Burke, brooding with power and terror, although Lugosi was already sleepwalking on his long decline from his height as Dracula.

History also made the undead part of haunted castles. Even outside the legends of King Vlad the Impaler and Dracula and vampires in Transylvanian castles, the gothic tradition of _The Monk_ onwards always peopled ruined keeps and windy battlements and cobwebbed cellars with evil spirits and resurrected torturers. Christopher Lee appeared in one of the films in this tradition as Count Drago, who turned his guests into instant statues by giving them a drug. Other victims could be tormented for his pleasure in the vaults before being petrified. And, naturally, in a picture amiably and literally entitled, _Castle of the Living Dead,_ coffins could not be far away as the storage chambers of the stoned people.

The most gothic cinema of all, the Italian horror movie, enjoyed putting its favourite screen vamp, Barbara Steele, into the role of the undead. Perhaps her most famous performance was in _Mask of the Demon,_ where she was nastily disfigured by an executioner's spiked mask clamped onto her face before being burned alive — luckily, she was as beautiful and voluptuous as ever when she revived in more modern times.

Above: Lee watches with pleasure the agonies of his tortured victims.
Below: The petrified undead are put into coffin storage in *Castle of the Living Dead.*

LE MASQUE
DU DÉMON

In *Castle of Blood*, however, she played a ghostly blood-sucking lady in a strange film where Edgar Allan Poe suddenly appeared, betting his guest that he would not survive the night in a castle that lived on human gore.

However rational we may be in these safer urban times, we can never suppress our ancient fears of the undead. We can never know if spirits may not come back to haunt us — even if it is only our unquiet consciences doing the haunting. We may be scared in graveyards, that the earth will open and give forth its contents before the day of judgement. Inanimate things, from puppets to statues, may suddenly develop a life of their own and attack us. In cemeteries and in prophecies, in antiquities and in memories, superstition lurks and troubles our souls. We live in the houses of the dead, we inhabit the cities which the dead made. What they have done, we see and feel and touch. Perhaps they can still inhabit their old places. Perhaps they can be called back to them, and we will see in the mirror their acts, and not our own.

Poe and guest remark on the pale vampire victim in *Castle of Blood*.

Barbara Steele eyes a victim in *Castle of Blood* (1964).

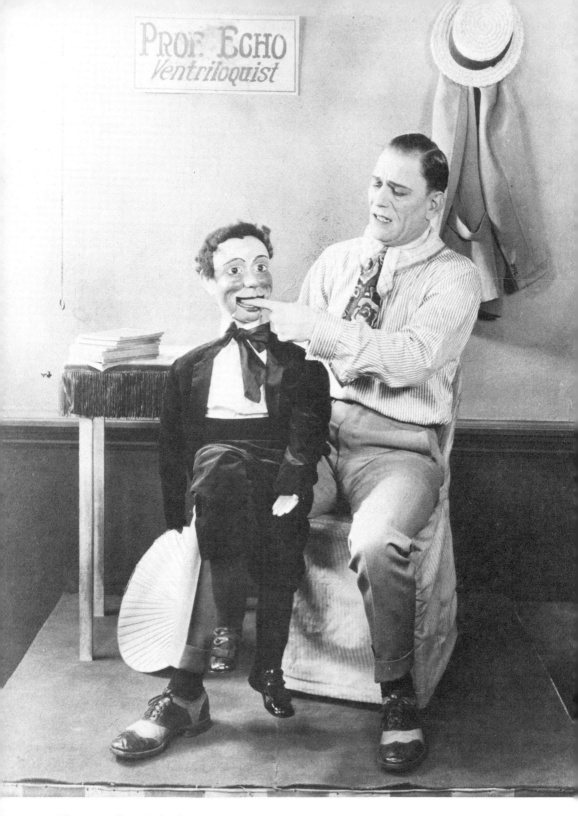

The ventriloquist's dummy comes
alive and bites Lon Chaney in Tod
Browning's *The Unholy Three* (1925).

The mirror makes people relive past crimes in *Dead of Night* (1945). There is also a living ventriloquist's dummy in this classic British horror film.

THE CULT OF THE COFFIN

Being buried alive was an obsession with Edgar Allan Poe. In his story, 'The Premature Burial', he wrote of awakening in the berth of a dark ship's cabin and, forgetting where he was, feeling the wooden box above, below, at his head, to one side, and knowing that he had been interred too soon. This fear was the basis of one of Roger Corman's films in his Poe cycle, *The Premature Burial*, with Ray Milland playing the man scared of being buried while in a cataleptic trance, then finding this true and coming back from

the dead to revenge himself on his family after grave-robbers had dug him up. Another version of the story, *The Oblong Box,* has the merit of featuring Vincent Price, whose elegance cannot save us from the horror of his disfigured brother getting out of his grave, where he should have gone on lying for our own good.

Poe concentrated on the cult of the cof-

Ray Milland is buried alive in a cataleptic trance in Corman's *The Premature Burial* (1962).

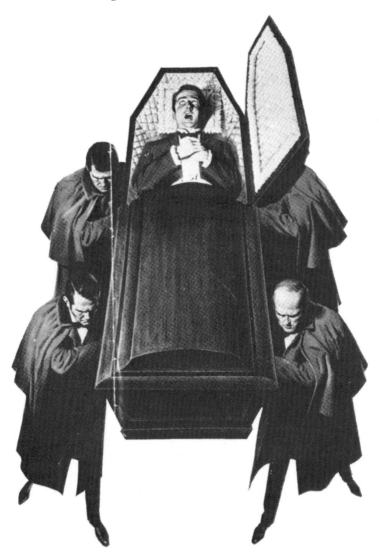

fin and the grave. In another story, 'Ligeia', he told of a first wife who refused to die when her body did, but returned in the person of the second wife. She had told her husband, after all, on her death-bed: 'Man doth not yield him to the angels, *nor unto death utterly,* save only through the weakness of his feeble will', Corman's version of this Poe tale has the Lady Ligeia coming back from resting not in peace over and over again, like a punch-drunk boxer who simply will not lie down for the count. However often her black coffin is put into her white mar-ble tomb, she will not accept it as a last resting place.

Yet Poe's most haunting story of the undead was 'The Fall of the House of Usher'. In it, Roderick Usher tells his guest that he may have buried his sister alive while she was in a trance. *'We have put her living in the tomb!'* he asserts. 'Said I not that my senses were acute? I *now* tell you that I heard her first feeble movements in the hollow coffin. I heard

Ligeia's coffin is put hopefully into her tomb in Corman's film.

them — many, many days ago — yet I dared not — *I dared not speak!* And now — tonight . . . will she not be here anon? Is she not hurrying to upbraid me for my haste? Have I not heard her footsteps on the stair? . . . MADMAN! I TELL YOU THAT SHE NOW STANDS WITHOUT THE DOOR!'

She has, indeed, broken open the lid of her coffin with her scrabbling and bleeding fingers, and she has come back emaciated to seek vengeance on her brother. In her death agony, she clutches him to her, while the guest flees through the mists and the lightning. Behind him, the House of Usher splits open and disappears in the black marsh.

As well as an obsession with premature burial and the endless return of the dead, Poe also feared ancient places haunted by evil spirits. Corman picked up a poem of Poe's called 'The Haunted Palace'. It dealt with a king who lived in a green land, but evil things in robes of sorrow surrounded him, and he died. Vast forms then moved behind the red-lit windows of his empty palace, and strange sounds came from it. At last, a hideous throng came out of its doors. So Corman was inspired to create his village of deformed

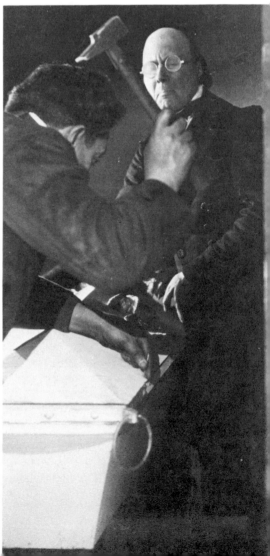

Roderick Usher and his guest seal the Lady Madeline in her coffin after laying her out with garlands in Jean Epstein's French version of *The Fall of the House of Usher,* made in 1928.

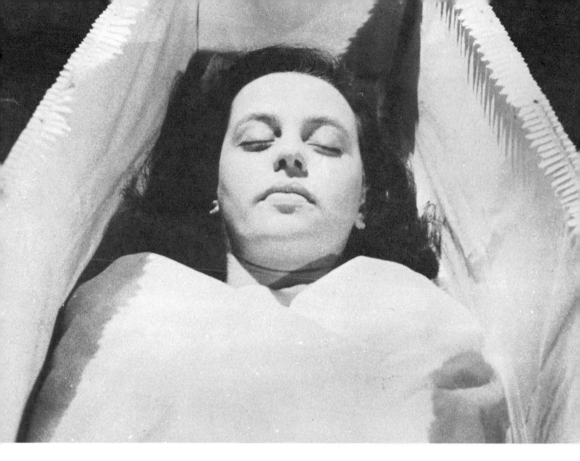

Above: The Lady Madeline is laid in her coffin more barely in a British version of *The House of Usher* of 1947 . . . *Below:* And her hand forces open the sealed coffin lid as she comes back from the dead.

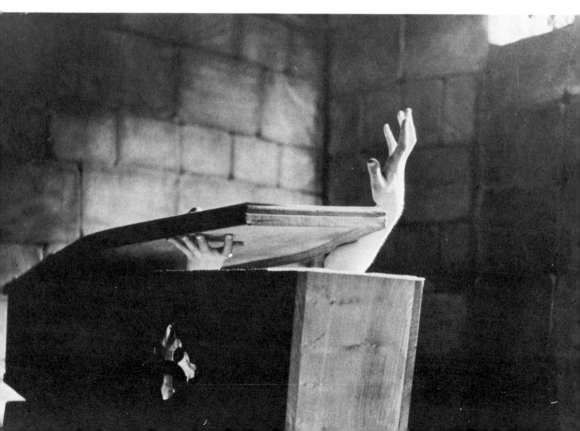

Above: The descendent of the warlock and his mistress, played by Vincent Price, digs at their grave . . . *Below:* And he causes their coffins to be lifted out of the cemetery in Corman's *The Haunted Palace* (1967).

Above: Boris Karloff pulls the stake out of John Carradine, playing an aristocratic Dracula in his velvet coffin in *House of Frankenstein* (1944). *Below:* the disfigured chemist is discovered in his resting place in *Castle of Evil* (1966).

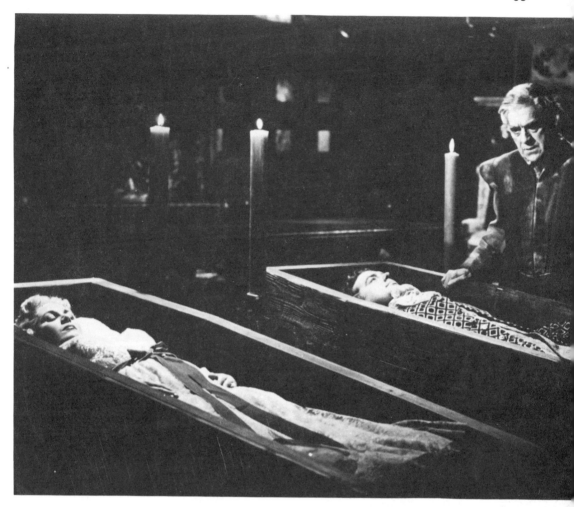

Boris Karloff and Lon Chaney Jr.
stayed among the coffins in *The Black
Castle* (1952).

mutants created by the spirit of a warlock and his mistress, which a later descendant dug up to exorcise. For the undead and the unquiet like to return to the place of their evil doings.

The cult of the coffin did not end with Poe. For it was always the place where the undead rested until they rose again. As John Donne's couplet went:

*The grave's a fine and private place
But none, I think, do there embrace.*

What some did there was to conserve their energy until they were called back to earth again, particularly the reincarnations of Dracula, who often seemed to like velvet linings to his later coffins rather than the original boxes of earth from Transylvania, in which the first Count made his voyage to Whitby.

A comfortable coffin, too, for the disfigured scientist in *Castle of Evil* In this strange concoction, the chemist with a horrible face slept in his pillowed box while his robot replica wandered about the castle killing off his heirs. In his case, the undead was a machine under his control, a mechanical zombie. Still in the gothic and Poe-like tradition were the plain wooden coffins of *The Black Castle*, where Boris Karloff pretended to look surprised to find living corpses inside them — actually, the corpses were merely full of a drug that left them in a death-like sleep. But the stone slab had to be

Barbara Steele is both inside and outside the slab in *The Long Hair of Death* (1964).

The galloping hearse and runaway coffin in *Entr'acte* (1924) . . .

. . . And the mourners racing after the dead.

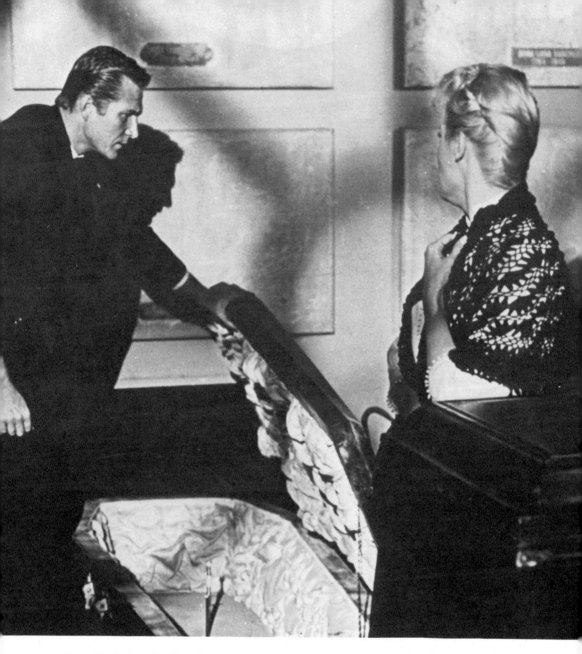

removed to find the dead-and-alive body
in *The Long Hair of Death*, in which the
ineffable Barbara Steele played a woman
wrongly burned at the stake for murder,
but coming back to life to save her
daughter from marrying the true murderer by trapping him in an effigy and
having him toasted to a crisp in his turn.

My favourite use of the coffin cult in
the cinema appears in René Clair's
surrealist comedy, *Entr'acte,* in which all
the far-out intellectuals of Paris break into a mad run to keep up with a runaway
hearse and coffin on their way to the

**The minister discovers the vampire
gunman's comfortable coffin in *Curse
of the Undead* (1959).**

cemetery. The coffin is also used stylishly
in two translations of the Dracula myth
to America. In *Curse of the Undead*, the
minister discovers the padded resting-
place, complete with spike, of the blood-
drinking gunslinger, who can only be shot
down by a bullet notched with a cross.
Even better was Francis Lederer's
smooth playing of a Southern Californian
Dracula in *The Fantastic Disappearing*

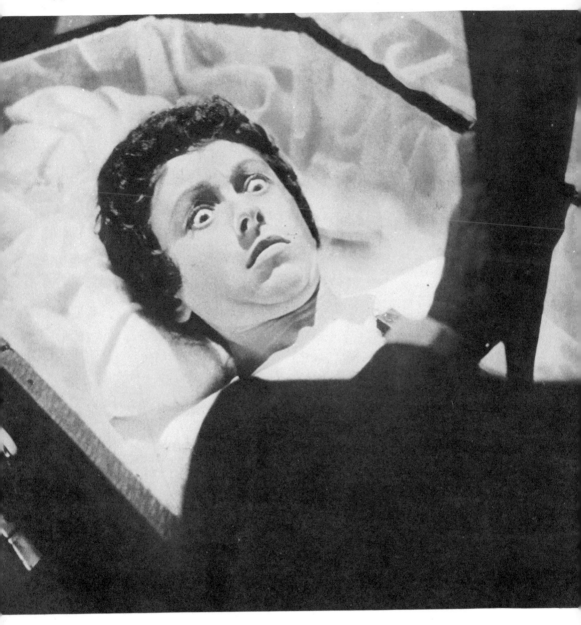

Francis Lederer wakes up in Southern California in *The Fantastic Disappearing Man,* **sometimes called** *The Return of Dracula* **(1957).**

Man. The coffin in that extravaganza was a real magician's box of tricks. Lederer made it appear uncomfortable to wake up in, and given the orgy of blood-drinking to follow, it was evident that he got out of the wrong side of his coffin that evening.

But he could do a marvellous vanishing trick in it, so that his body dematerialised in the daytime to the astonishment of the sheriff and of the coroner's office. He could also metamorphose himself into mist or a bat or a werewolf in his coffinful of surprises. It was bad luck on him that he slipped into a pit by mistake and impaled himself on a stake. It could happen to the most careful of vampires.

In *Macabre,* the coffin was used falsely

Above: The sheriff and the coroner are puzzled by the disappearance of the body in *The Fantastic Disappearing Man. **Below:** Lederer disappears into mist, also changes into a bat and a werewolf in *The Fantastic Disappearing Man.*

The tomb and the skeleton are props for the Devil in *The Satanists* (1970).

to terrify a man to death by persuading him that his young and beloved daughter had been buried alive. The coffin remains a symbol of horror and the devil — empty, it can be more terrifying than full. What *was* in it can be worse than what *is* in it! Certainly, in two films about the cult of witchcraft, *The Hand of Night* and *The Satanists*, coffins and tombs and skeletons are part of the necessary trappings of the cult of the devil without the need

The coffins are part of a satanic cult in *The Hand of Night* (1966).

for anyone to be in them. And in the sad effort to make de Sade's *Justine*, she was served up to her torturer on top of a tomb, but even that failed to excite very much.

Yet even the coffin can have its lighter moments. In Julien Duvivier's remarkable *The Curse and the Coffin*, the body lying in its bier appears and disappears to the most unlikely places. On one occasion, it flies into the middle of a tea-dance, which hardly knew that it was celebrating a wake. But perhaps the most inventive use of the coffin was in the stupendously camp Peter Cushing film, *The Skull*. In that strange movie, de Sade enters again as his own skull, dug out of his red-lined coffin and brought in by a collector. The skull has the power of floating and levitating objects, as well as driving the poor collector to murder. Poor de Sade! The producers were lucky to get away with it, for the de Sade family is proud of the ancient noble name and successfully sued the *Marat-Sade* theatre production in Paris for putting out a poster linking the family name with a notorious revolutionary like Marat.

So the cult of the coffin, begun by Poe, continues to haunt the screen. In fact, the modern wide screen is shaped like a coffin itself, an oblong box which reminds us very well of the final box where we shall all end — unless we have to rise from the dead again at some cry of 'Action!'

Above: Even lying on a tomb fails to make the naked lady very interesting in *Justine* (1972). **Below:** The corpse appears lying in state in the middle of the tea-dance in *The Curse of the Coffin* (1961).

BLOOD FOR THE DEAD

The double mark of the vampire's fangs is on the victim's throat in Jess Franco's *La Fille du Diable* (1965).

In the age of saving lives through blood transfusion, vampires are not so old-fashioned as they used to be. In cases where a patient has his blood-stream infected, more than ten pints a day of fresh blood have to be circulated through his veins — quite enough to make Dracula think that he had a hangover. The method of slowly infusing blood by two drip-feeds into the veins is remarkably similar to the double bite of the vampire's fangs — and if the vampire drinks blood instead of injecting it into the body, we must remember that the blood given to a patient is drawn from other people. In fact, there are many hospital vampires among us, who literally owe their lives to the blood of others. At Hastings in Sussex, apparently, a devil cult robbed the local blood bank. It was the easiest way of getting hold of human gore in a good state for their black masses.

There is a trend in vampire movies to recognise the connection between the hospital and the blood-sucker — and it is not only a question of gouging out of patients high medical fees. In an early Bogart feature, *The Return of Dr X,* he played a man who had been in the electric chair, but who needed fresh blood daily to stay alive a second time round. Modern vampires used hypodermic needles rather than fangs.

In a more old-fashioned way, the laboratory provided the blood supply for Gianna Maria Canale in *Lust of the Vampire.* She was certainly beautiful enough, pausing on the stairway of her cobwebbed castle, to make a man yield a pint or two of best rhesus negative for the pleasure of her youth and company. Unfortunately, like many a lady vampire, she did not know when to stop. As Daniel Massey

Humphrey Bogart (centre) wears rimless spectacles in *The Return of Dr. X* (1939), but somehow fails to appear scholarly.

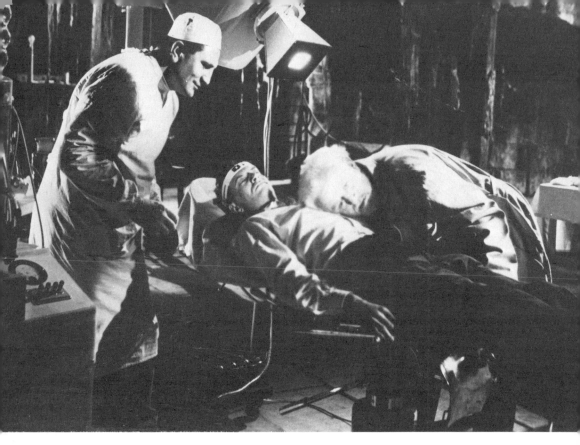

Above: The blood supply is prepared in *Lust of the Vampire* (1956). *Below:* Gianna Maria Canale vets the victim from the staircase of her castle.

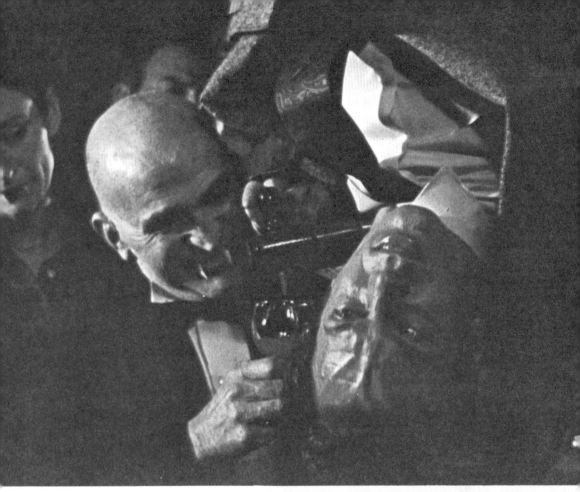

Daniel Massey (right) is tapped like a wine barrel by the vampires in their restaurant in _Vault of Horror_ (1974).

found out in _Vault of Horrors_ once a vampire group began using him as a cask of gore — they drained him dry too fast.

The vampire film had begun as a country matter. The original vampire Count, Max Schreck in _Nosferatu_, came out of a castle in Transylvania, travelled in an earth box and a sailing ship, and looked like something out of a circus freak show, not a laboratory. Bela Lugosi, playing the vampire, was always elegant in his approach, a dandy about drinking blood. A certain modesty always enveloped even the victims of the vampires in those decent days of the early cinema. The marks of the blood-letting were shown, but not seen. The gore did not appear. Blood was not yet box-office.

Max Schreck comes out of his castle in _Nosferatu_ (1922).

Above: Lugosi and vampire helper approach their victim elegantly in *Mark of the Vampire* (1935). *Below:* Conrad Nagel (right) points to the place where the vampire strikes in *London After Midnight* (1927). In fact, the vampires prove to be false in this discreet Tod Browning movie.

Above: Elizabeth Allen hides the double puncture in front of Lionel Barrymore in Browning's sequel, *Mark of the Vampire* (1935). Again the vampire proves to be a red herring. *Below:* Sandra Harrison attacks her victim in *Blood Is My Heritage.*

her eyes
DESIRE!

her veins the
od of a .....
MONSTER!

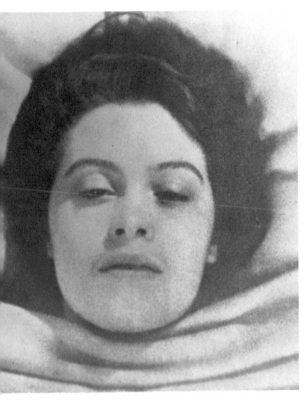

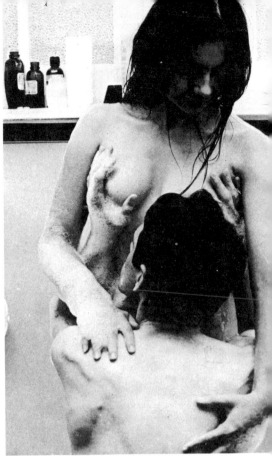

Above left: Dreyer's vampire girl is discretion herself under the sheets. *Above right:* The Bloody Fairy is indiscretion herself in the shower as she prepares her victim for the bite.

HANNAH
Queen of the Vampires

THE CURSE OF THE VAMPIRE

SHE'S WAITING TO LOVE YOU...TO DEATH

Climax
after
climax
of
terror
and
desire...

where the living
change places
with the dead.

IN
METROCOLOR

THE
VELVET VAMPIRE

Yet as the cult of the vampire grew, so the blood began to show as the undead filled themselves up from their victims. The fangs began to protrude like scalpels. Sandra Harrison looked like a sabre-toothed tigress in *Blood Is My Heritage,* otherwise known as *Blood of Dracula* and made in 1957. It was hypnosis which turned her into a vampire monster. Yet she was a bloodbath away from the discreet girl vampire of Dreyer's *Vampyr* of 1931, just as she was nothing like the titillating slaughterhouse of *The Bloody Fairy* of 1968.

Two monarchs of the vampires fought for the right to be the most powerful of them all. One was Hannah, self-styled Queen of the Vampires, whose teeth made *Jaws* look like a love-bite. The other was the female blood-drinking alien in Roger Corman's *Queen of Blood,* who died of a small cut and left some eggs laid behind her to hatch out her heirs. *(See Colour Section)* The bites of the other vampire ladies, however, got more and more like massacres. *The Curse of the Vampire* seemed to set a new record for gore running down the celluloid, but soon it was to be put to shame by the bloodiest vampire lady of them all, *The Velvet Vampire* of 1971, who liked waving the severed heads of her victims in the air.

THE NUDE VAMPIRE

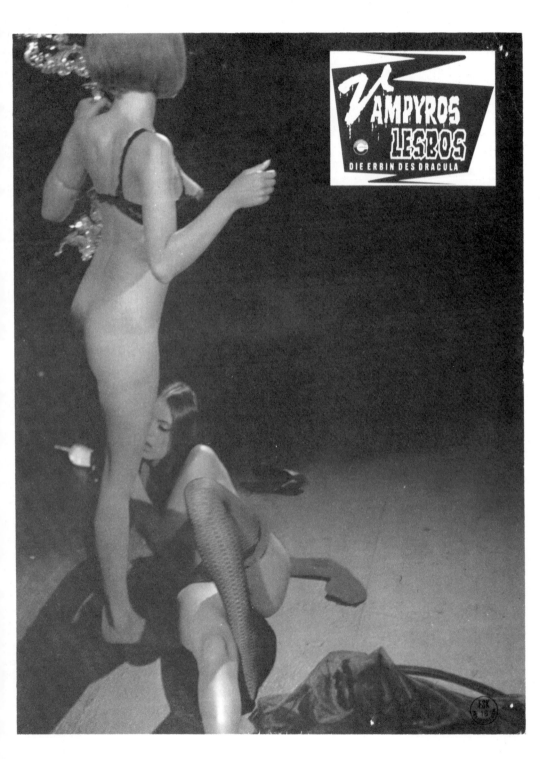

VAMPYROS
LESBOS
DIE ERBIN DES DRACULA

John Carradine spreads his bat-cloak as wide as he can in *House of Dracula* (1945).

Where blood flowed, sex followed. First of all, Dracula's victims became more and more naked, as Christopher Lee swooped his dark and handsome way across the screen. In a series of naked vampire movies, Jean Rollin set his sights as low as soft pornography and achieved something like camp success with a picture actually called *The Nude Vampire*. But perhaps the best of the titles of the sex-and-blood lady vampire concoctions was *Vampyros Lesbos,* one of Jess Franco's run-of-the-can quick movies — it was also entitled *The Heiress of Dracula.* She was the Count's descendant in her taste for blood, but her sexual tastes were all her own modern invention.

The male vampires simply could not keep up with all this titillation and stripping. They could bare their fangs even wider than the women, but baring their breasts was out. They could only open their batwing cloaks even wider, or be surrounded by a court of beautiful girl blood-suckers as in *The Empire of Dracula.* They could become African prin-

Left: German Robles plays the fanged vampire Count for the Spanish-speaking world.

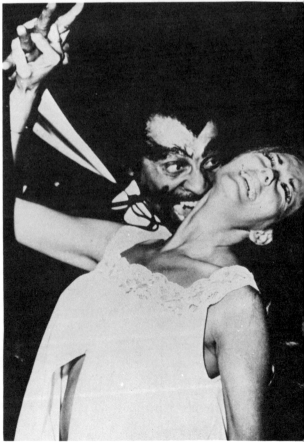

Blacula bites the neck of his victim in 1974.

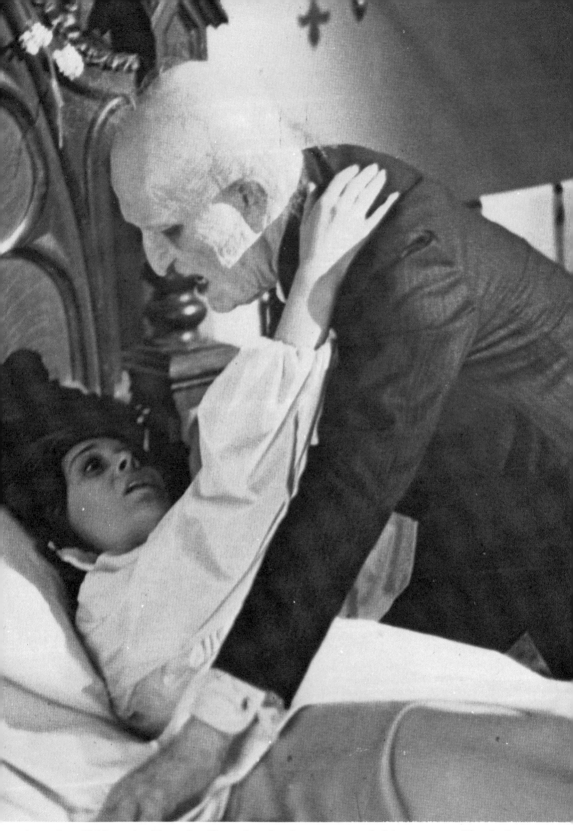

Jonathan Frid as the Vampire Barnabas is almost too arthritic to gnaw his victim in *House of Dark Shadows* (1970).

cely vampires such as Blacula, trying to put some colour into a lifeless genre. They could leap into the martial arts to give a kick to the blood-sucking males. But generally, all we can say of the recent men vampires is that women's liberation has been out for blood on the screen, and that the male Draculas Minor are dying off of old age and anaemia, like the geriatric Barnabas of *House of Dark Shadows.*

In fact, the only way the male gore-seekers from the undead could fight back from the monstrous horde of girl vampires was to make themselves look even more tortured and unhappy than they usually did with the traditional stake through their heart. They had to look even more repulsive than re-animated corpses — certainly they had been underground too long. Gone was the aristocratic and pale Lugosi figure. Out of the Philippines came perhaps the most beastly and corrupt of the vampires; the tropics really seemed to have got at his complexion.

In the end, the elegant blood-sucker had to go under the disfigurement of the laboratory to become interesting to a younger generation, inured to horrific sights and scientific jargon. In one advertisement for a double bill, *Brain of Blood* and *Vampire People*, we can see the new bestial maniac from the surgeon's paw leap to top billing above the reduced and cloaked vampire Count of the good old days. The teasers to tempt people into the cinemas were still horrific, but more scientific. The catchlines were:

A BLOOD-DRIPPING BRAIN
TRANSPLANT TURNS A
MANIAC INTO A MONSTER!
HIS BODY DIED, HIS
BRAIN WAS SAVED FOR THE
MOST UNHOLY
EXPERIMENTS!
SCIENCE MEETS HORROR
AS A MAN-MADE CREATURE
COMES ALIVE!
BLOOD AND BRAIN SERUM
MIX IN A SPECTACLE OF
SHOCKING HORROR!

That might be all right for *Brain of Blood,* but even the *Vampire People* had to be updated with the catchline:

THE VAMPIRES FIND NEW
VICTIMS TO FEED THEIR
ROTTED CORPSES!
INNOCENT YOUNG GIRLS
SUPPLY THE LIFE-GIVING
POWERS OF PLASMA!

The undead are nastier and more medical than they used to be.

DOUBLE DOSE OF SHOCK!
A Blood-dripping Brain Transplant turns a Maniac into a Monster...

all New!!! **BRAIN of BLOOD**

in blood-curdling color

STARRING KENT TAYLOR / GRANT WILLIAMS / REED HADLEY / REGINA CARROL

AND
A cult of Undead Creatures seek fresh warm Human Blood!

VAMPIRE PEOPLE

IN COLOR!

GP

© HEMISPHERE PICTURES, INC.

THE WALKING HORRORS

If vampires increasingly left the castle for the laboratory and the bat-cloak for the bosom, zombies also soon left their original voodoo islands and became the creatures of mad scientists, the walking dead without will, the instruments of the revenge of insane researchers. The first anatomical experiments consisted in examining the dead to try and find the secrets of life, and the first experiments in making dead matter move were by primitive electrical means. On one famous occasion, recorded by Mary Shelley in her original *Frankenstein*, an electric shock made the severed leg of a frog twitch into motion.

After his roles as Frankenstein's Monster and the Mummy, Karloff seemed the natural actor to play ghouls, zombies and the undead. In 1933, he made his first British horror picture, called *The Ghoul*. It relied heavily on the plot of *The Mummy*, with a sacred stolen jewel causing the dead Egyptologist Professor Morlant, played by Karloff, to rise again from the dead to revenge himself.

Although the plot of the film was slow, Karloff saved it by his acting and make-up. 'He does resemble, even before his demise,' one American review said, 'something dead rather than alive. He gives a curiously supernatural impression always by the blankness in the eyes, and by that strange robot gait of his which seems to be directed by a mind outside himself.'

The blank look and the gait were again used frighteningly by Karloff in his curious satanic film with Lugosi of 1934, *The Black Cat*. Yet more effective was his part in *The Walking Dead* of 1936. In that, he plays the part of a man wrongly electrocuted for murder, then brought back to life by the latest in electrical methods. Once revived, Karloff visits each of the true racketeer murderers in turn and frightens them to death, before returning to the dead himself after warning the scientist who had revived him against repeating any further experiments in resurrection.

This walking dead role was one which he was to repeat in *The Man They Could Not Hang* of 1939, except that he actually killed most of the jurors who had mistakenly sentenced him to death. In this second walkabout, it was a mechanical heart which brought him back

A 16th century woodcut of an early anatomical experiment.

Above: Boris Karloff as Professor Morlant shows the sacred jewel which must be buried with him in *The Ghoul. Below:* The mourners carry the corpse of Professor Morlant to his tomb.

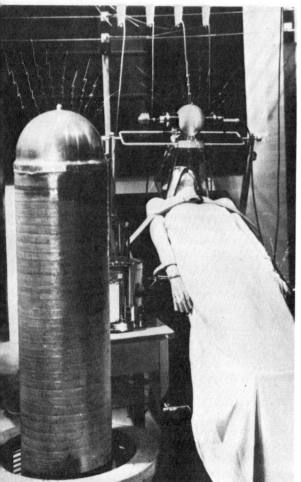

Karloff and Lugosi in the sinister *The Black Cat.*

to life, although it hung out of a plate in his chest in two glass globes.

Once typecast in his role of trying to communicate with the dead, Karloff could never leave it. In the interesting *The Devil Commands* of 1941, he claimed that the brainwaves of the dead remained behind them, and he used the old electrical spark gap to try to make living mediums talk to corpses excavated from the graveyard. It was the ancient body-snatcher in modern scientific disguise. So was next year's vehicle with Peter Lorre, *The Boogie Man Will Get You*, which had Karloff keeping five people in a state of suspended animation in his basement, trying to create the first Fascist 'super-man' — the Nazi terror was then high in America. He rightly ended in the insane asylum at the conclusion of the movie.

While no other actor equalled Karloff's genius at playing the undead, Lugosi had a try at it. The curious wooden quality of his acting, as though he were in a permanent drugged trance, had made *Dracula* a great success, but he could not translate it to his other films. The very

Modern electrical methods bring Karloff back to life in *The Walking Dead.*

Karloff returns to life for his revenge in _The Walking Dead_.

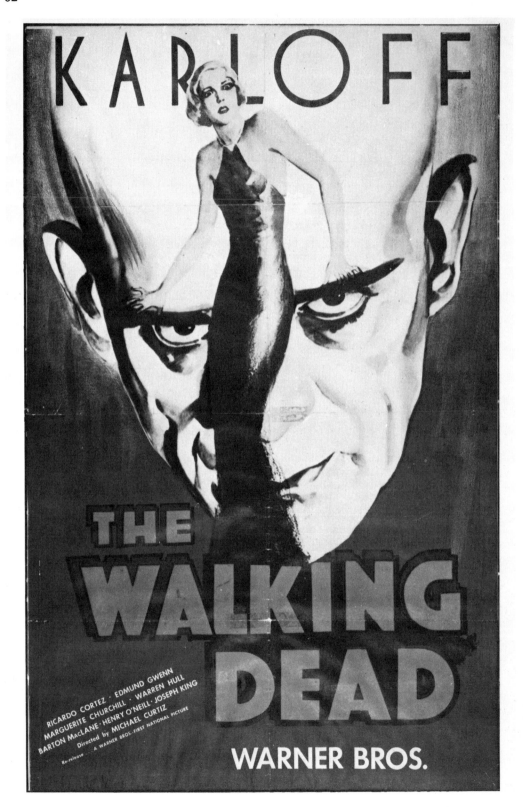

Above: Karloff and Ann Revere use an electrical experiment to show that brainwaves live on after death in *The Devil Commands.* **Below:** The corpse in a robot suit rather than a coffin tries to talk to Amanda Duff with Karloff holding the communicator.

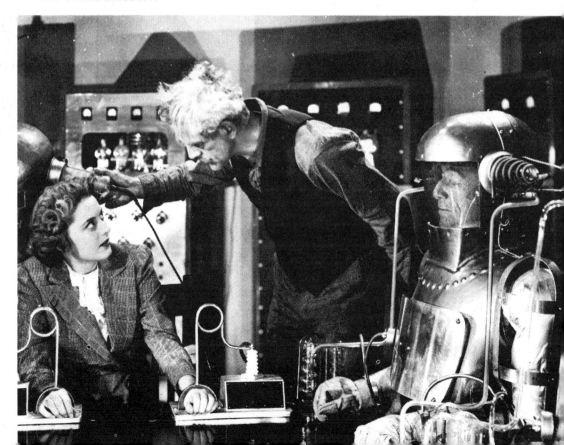

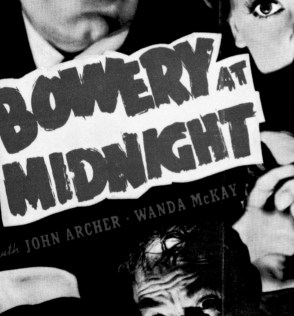

ASTOR PICTURES presents

BELA LUGOSI

BOWERY AT MIDNIGHT

with JOHN ARCHER · WANDA McKAY

HIDEOUS BEYOND BELIEF...with an INHUMAN CRAVING!

AMERICAN INTERNATIONAL'S

QUEEN of BLOOD

IN **PATHÉCOLOR**

STARRING

JOHN SAXON · BASIL RATHBONE · JUDI MEREDITH

THE GRAVE CAN'T HOLD IT
...nothing human can stop it!

...it rose from the crypt to slake its monstrous thirst for beauty...*and the power to rule the earth!*

THE **THING** THAT **COULDN'T DIE**

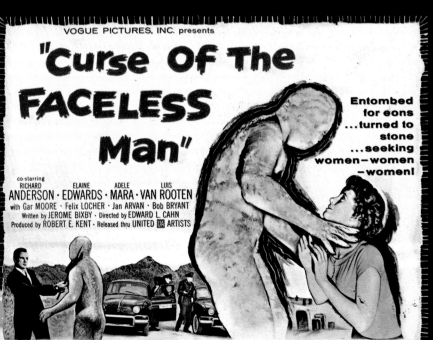

SUPERNATURAL UNDERSEA THRILLS!

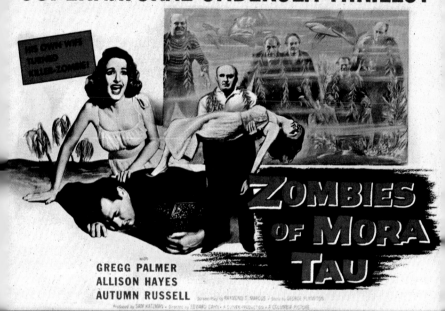

HIS OWN WIFE TURNED KILLER-ZOMBIE!

ZOMBIES OF MORA TAU

with
GREGG PALMER
ALLISON HAYES
AUTUMN RUSSELL

Screen Play by RAYMOND T. MARCUS · Story by GEORGE PLYMPTON
Produced by SAM KATZMAN · Directed by EDWARD CAHN · A CLOVER PRODUCTION · A COLUMBIA PICTURE

"THE **FOUR SKULLS** OF **JONATHAN DRAKE**"

Your Money NOT Refunded If You Faint!

This Picture Was Written, Produced and Directed to SCARE THE DAYLIGHTS OUT OF YOU!

He was custodian of the icebox that kept the skulls crisp and fresh!

THE DOCTOR WHO IS ALWAYS COOKING UP SOME FRIGHTENING SKULLDUGGERY!

co-starring
EDUARD FRANZ
VALERIE FRENCH
GRANT RICHARDS · **HENRY DANIELL**
Written by ORVILLE H. HAMPTON · Directed by EDWARD L. CAHN · Produced by ROBERT E. KENT
A VOGUE PICTURES, INC. Presentation · Released thru UNITED ARTISTS

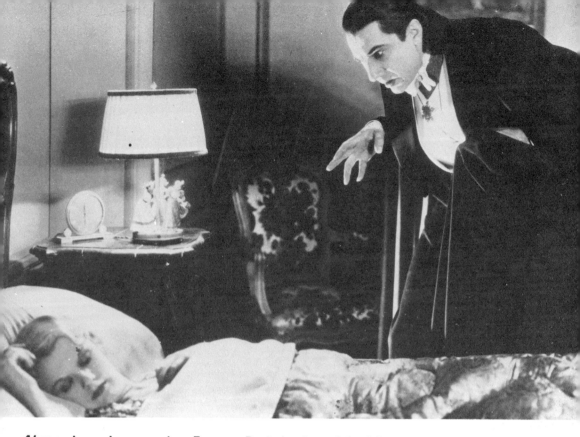

Above: Lugosi approaches Frances Dade in the original *Dracula* (1932).
Below: In *Return of the Vampire* (1944) Lugosi was already sleep-walking through his elegant vampire role. Here he approaches Nina Foch.

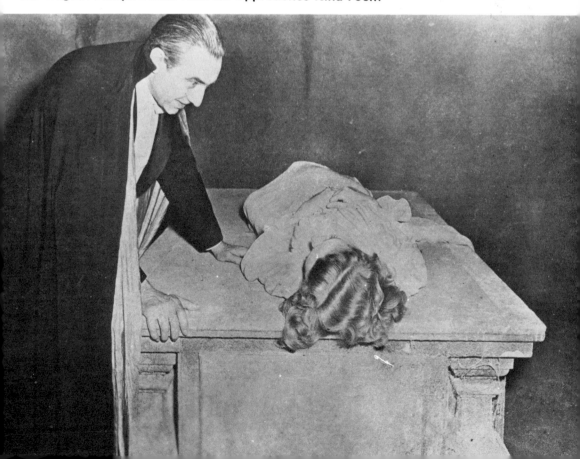

Above: Here the declining Lugosi tries to play his famous Dracula role seriously in *Abbott and Costello Meet Frankenstein* (1948). He still had just enough dignity not to appear ridiculous. *Below:* Lugosi disassociates himself from being trapped by the Dead End Kids.

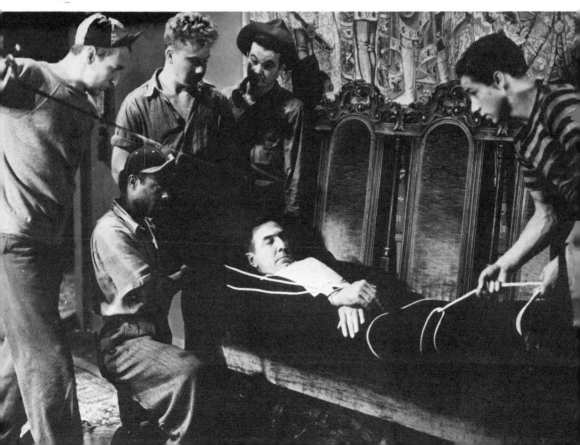

sloth of his performance, which had instilled terror in Dracula's castle as he crept upon his victims, induced boredom later. When he kept to his aristocratic dressing-gowns and evening clothes, he had a certain stately magnificence like a gothic mansion on the verge of crumbling into ruin. Yet as his acting performance petrified and his box-office appeal diminished, he descended into ridiculous roles. The most farcical of them was his playing of the well-dressed killer in *Spooks Run Wild*, when he set himself up as a straight man for the Dead End Kids.

Lugosi's great mistake was ever to leave his elegant dress which excused his sleepwalker's gait. In *Dead Men Walk*, the aging Lugosi played a black magician, determined to outlive his death.

That he did, successfully returning from beyond the grave as a vampire with superhuman powers. Unfortunately, his costume did not survive his journey in and out of existence. If the worms didn't get him, the moths did. When he came to a final clash with a surprised George Zucco wearing the trilby of the period and using a chair to fend Lugosi off, Lugosi only looked dishevelled and distraught rather than deadly and dangerous.

In one film of his decline, *Bowery at Midnight*, Lugosi showed some of his early Dracula quality. There he played an evil genius who killed and then returned his victims to life as walking zombies who had to obey his will. *(See Colour Section)* Perhaps he liked the power of the situation, for the mad scientist role in control of the walking dead was superior to the role of the undead itself, groping around somnambulistically. Even the great Erich von Stroheim had played the mad surgeon in later roles, particularly in *The Crime of Doctor Crespi* of 1935. In that, he gave a rival doctor a paralysing drug and had him buried alive. Fortunately, his victim recovered from being a zombie under Stroheim's control, unlike the subject of another Stroheim brain experiment in *The Lady and the Monster* of 1944.

Lugosi as the black magician shows his powers to George Zucco in *Dead Men Walk* (1942).

Zucco wins the showdown with the
unkempt Lugosi, back from the grave
in *Dead Men Walk*.

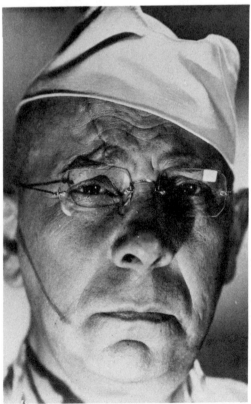

As with the vampire, the laboratory
became the place to drain blood and
create zombies. Even when old-fashioned
coffins were brough into shot, a hypodermic was a better tool for resurrection
than a spade. In *The Black Sleep*, the
deformed zombies were the creatures of
drugs rather than magic or nightmares.
Hospital beds were good places to create
inhumans, who killed from the fear of
eternal loneliness as in *The Night of the
Devils*. In one of the few vehicles to unite
the horror talents of Vincent Price and
Christopher Lee and Peter Cushing,
Scream and Scream Again of 1969, this
'triple-distilled horror as powerful as a
vat of boiling acid' mixed up Dracula with

Erich von Stroheim used his
considerable powers of terror and
hypnotic skill in 'mad doctor' roles,
creating zombies from his patients to
do his wicked will.

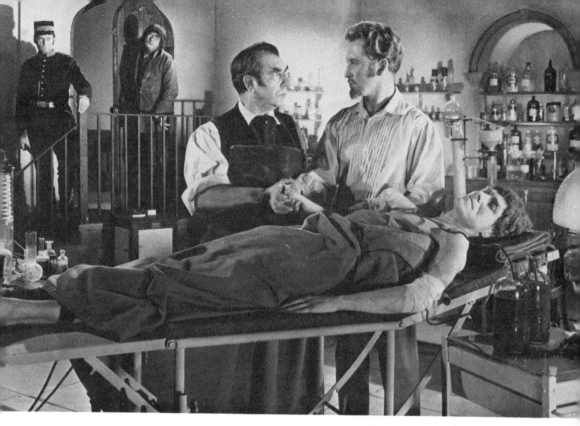

Above: Sir Donald Wolfit plays the anaemic and blood-needing doctor in *Blood of the Vampire* (1958). *Below:* In *The Black Sleep* or *Dr Cadman's Secret* (1956), a death-in-life malforming drug was used by Basil Rathbone (right) on his victims. He is here seen talking to Akim Tamiroff.

Frankenstein in modern laboratory conditions, so that a host of vampire supermen androids were discovered bloodsucking the city dry in a plot to take over the world. It was a meeting of old themes in new clinical surroundings, which did not quite synthesise correctly.

Methods of creating zombies and nightmare creatures were limited. There was decapitation or transplants of the head. *The Thing That Couldn't Die* was a black magician's head chopped off in Elizabethan times, which was rediscovered in a sealed casket. As the catchlines went:

'They chopped off its head and buried it for 400 years . . . yet it lives today!'

'Making every woman who stares into its evil eyes a willing slave — turning every man into a monster!'

'It rose from the crypt to slake its monstrous thirst for beauty . . . and the power to rule the earth.'

'Stare into its eyes - - if you dare!' *(See Colour Section)*

Boris Karloff also in *Black Sabbath* came riding in as a vampire Wurdalak with a severed head in his fist. But in *The Four Skulls of Jonathan Drake,* all the male members of the family died of decapitation at the age of sixty to fulfil the ancestral curse. One of the more unspeakable monsters of our time lurched across the screen representing a zombie with an ancient Drake skull sewn onto a corrupt witchdoctor's body. Luckily, at death, the heaving mass disintegrated into dust. *(See Colour Section)*

Drugs, of course, were the main way of turning men into the other side of their split personalities — they are still used, after all, in the clinical treatment of schizophrenia. All modern Jekyll and Hyde transformations depend on drugs rather than a change in psyche. If no actor has improved upon Frederic March playing the diabolic Mr Hyde, there were many *grand guignol* variations on the theme of man to monster. The most frightening of them is perhaps, Paul Naschy playing the wolfman in *Frankenstein's Bloody Terror,* which has nothing to do with Frankenstein and much to do with bloody terror. In it, we could 'see vic-

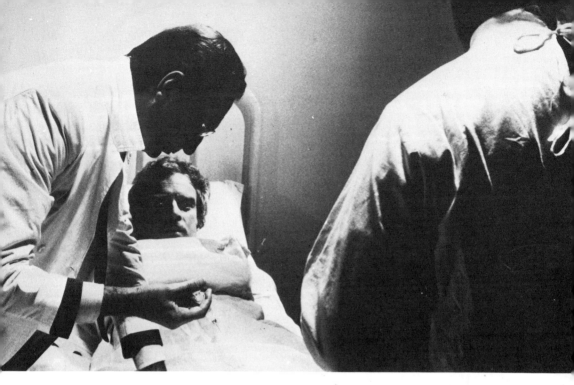

Above: The killers are created in *The Night of the Devils* (1971). *Below:* Vincent Price looks pained to be in the picture, or to have the scalpel at his throat in *Scream and Scream Again* (1969).

AN AMERICAN INTERNATIONAL PICTURE STARRING

VINCENT PRICE
CHRISTOPHER LEE
PETER CUSHING

TRIPLE DISTILLED HORROR
...as powerful as a vat of boiling ACID!

SCREAM AND SCREAM AGAIN

CO-STARRING JUDY HUXTABLE · ALFRED MARKS · MICHAEL GOTHARD

COLOR BY MOVIELAB

PRODUCED BY MAX ROSENBERG and MILTON SUBOTSKY · SCREENPLAY BY CHRISTOPHER WICKING · DIRECTED BY GORDON HESSLER

Frederic March is transformed into the
bestial Mr Hyde.

Not all mutants were lucky enough to
be transformed into hairy monsters. The
zombies made from experiments could
be turned into stone, like the 200-year-old
scientists who gradually petrified themselves after staying alive for centuries
through stealing energy from young
women. Yet stone was probably better for
a staggering zombie than soap-suds were.
The people transformed by the mad scientist in his Caribbean Cave of Death in
Unknown Terror came out as zombies ex-
panding in detergent bubbles, a sort of
soapy fungus that threatened to spread
over the whole globe. More human — and
more inhuman — were the atomic zombies controlled by radar and stomping
around like robots with the strength of
ten men in *Creature with the Atom Brain*,
a tribute to nuclear research rather than
good horror film-making. *(See Colour Section)*

tims horribly mutilated by the Walking
Dead!' But the funniest was the test-tube
monster created from a coelacanth's aged
fangs in *Monster on the Campus*, in which
Troy Donahue made a best-forgotten
early appearance.

**The doctor experimenting in creating
eternal life only manages to create *The
Unearthly* (1957).**

Fear of operations and of hospitals is
greater in us now than fear of zombies
and the undead. That is why the cinema
has tried to graft the two fears together.
They terrify us more. Perhaps if the
scalpel slips or the drug goes wrong, we
will emerge as human vegetables or a
creature under control of another's will.
The chemical or the knife may also make
us one of *The Unearthly* who were made
that way in 1957. For medicine is merely
the modern version of the witchdoctor's
craft.

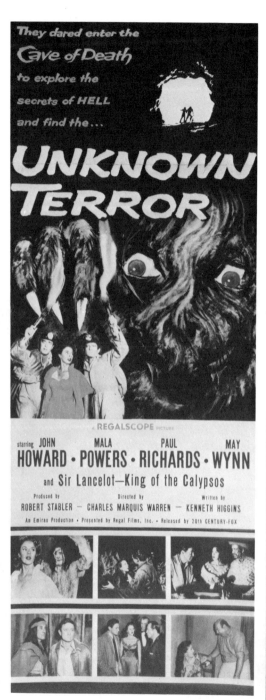

ZOMBIES

The original zombies came from witchcraft and magic, voodoo and rituals. In a strange Canadian film, *Eyes of Hell* or *The Mask,* the putting on of an ancient Aztec mask caused the hero to become a zombie, controlled by pre-Columbian thought, bent upon murder. It was the first case in the movies of early American savagery controlling a modern man, with the alien force deriving from the days before the Mayflower landed or the slave-ships imported voodoo to the New World.

All other pure zombie pictures, however, should originate in Haiti, where the voodoo witchdoctors are credited with bringing back the undead to act as their slaves without willpower. In 1932, the remarkable fantasy year of the making of *Dracula* and *King Kong,* a film called *White Zombie* was the prototype for all following zombie films. Bela

Made a zombie by putting on the Aztec mask, the murderer sets out.

Lugosi actually appeared in that film as well, playing 'Murder' Legendre, the master of the zombies, who was enlisted by the villian to use his zombie slaves to turn a good girl into a zombie to satisfy the villian's desires.

The zombies are first seen in the film as black silhouettes lurching down a hill, and Lugosi is first introduced by a close-up of his eyes, superimposed over his figure waiting for the unsuspecting travellers to approach in a coach driven by one of his zombies. Lugosi's role suited him as he had little dialogue and was wholly evil, and the producers, the Halperin brothers, made the film full of the slow ritual of death. An effort of theirs to make a sequel, *Revolt of the Zombies,* set in Cambodia in 1936, had none of the brooding stealth of *White Zombie* as in the sequence when Lugosi

The ancient Aztec death-mask possesses its worshippers in *Eyes of Hell* (1961).

sends the girl under his power off to do her first murder for him.

The next time a zombie was used in a movie was for comedy thrills. Noble Johnson played the threatening figure from the living dead in *The Ghost Breakers,* a vehicle for the young Bob Hope and Paulette Goddard, set in Cuba rather than Haiti. It was neither very scary nor very funny as a movie; but it was remade in 1952 as a Dean Martin and Jerry Lewis vehicle under the title of *Scared Stiff,* and it was successful enough to start a run of zombie movies during the Second World War, possibly because the sending overseas of millions of American men to tropical islands made those that stayed at

Left: Madge Bellamy in the grip of a zombie in *White Zombie* (1932). *Above:* A zombie drives Robert Frazer on his way to meet Lugosi, playing 'Murder' Legendre. Frazer, who will become a zombie, draws out one of Lugosi's best lines, 'Well, well, we understand one another *better* now'. *Below:* Bela Lugosi turns Madge Bellamy into a zombie and sends her off on a killing mission, watched by the new zombie Robert Frazer. *Right:* Noble Johnson plays the zombie in the comedy horror film, *The Ghost Breakers,* as he terrifies Bob Hope and Paulette Goddard in 1940.

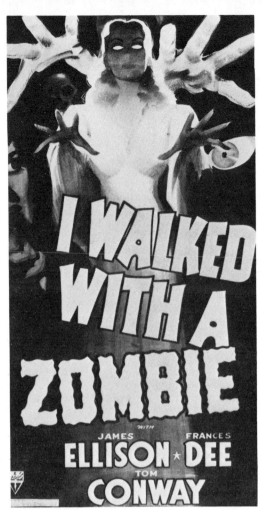

home want to fantasise about the perils waiting for their men out there.

There is little to be said about the two 1941 zombie pictures, *King of the Zombies* and *Love Wanga*, except that the zombies are used as spies by foreign agents in the first film and to excite the heroine — not the audience — in the second. Val Lewton, however, redeemed the zombie movie from silliness with his extraordinary movie about voodoo in Haiti, *I Walked With a Zombie* of 1943. He based the plot on *Jane Eyre* and on a series of newspaper articles about voodoo on the Caribbean island. The pacing of the film is full of exquisite terror, from the time that the nurse and her half-zombie patient see a gigantic silent black man to their view of a voodoo doll hanging from the branch of a tree.

Thereafter, the plot thickens and quickens. Men are attacked by forces unknown and carried back. The patient remains possessed like a zombie, and nothing can be done for her by the most modern treatment. If not quite as haunting as Lewton's *The Cat People*, his zombie film is another of his superb exercises

A victim of the zombies is brought inside in Lewton's film.

The two American girls are terrified by the appearance of a vast silent black man, perhaps a zombie . . . And by a hanging voodoo doll in Lewton's *I Walked With a Zombie.*

One of the American girls becomes a
white zombie in Lewton's film.

BURIED, ALIVE!

A beautiful girl on a
desolate isle...where
a monster that was
once a man...deals
out terrifying
tortures!

BORIS KARLOFF
IN
ISLE OF THE DEAD

with ELLEN DREW
MARC CRAMER

RKO RADIO

Produced by VAL LEWTON · Directed by MARK ROBSON · Written by Ardel Wray

in suggesting terror without slapping the
audience in the face with it like a wet rag
in a fairground Haunted House.

Lewton went on to use the theme of the
undead in his curious film with Boris
Karloff of 1945, *Isle of the Dead*. In that
odd tale of a woman buried alive like a
Poe heroine and a crazed general played
by Karloff, the atmosphere is stronger
than the action. It is all mood and little
moment. It was nearly the end of
Lewton's career as a major master of
horror films.

In the same year of *I Walked With a
Zombie*, that underrated lead actor of
terror, John Carradine, played in a little
movie called *Revenge of the Zombies*. Its
plot was run-of-the-blood, although it was
updated by the war. A doctor operating
the swamplands of the Deep South tried
to create an army of invincible zombies to
help the Nazis. He turned his wife into a
zombie to aid him, but she finally turned
the tables on him, taking control of the

Boris Karloff plays the brooding General Pherides in Val Lewton's *Isle of the Dead* (1945).

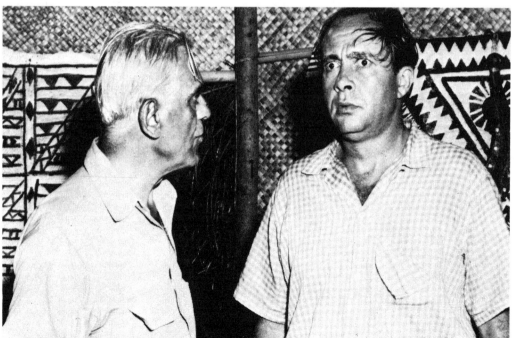

Karloff meets the zombie, played by Murvyn Vye, in *Voodoo Island.*

zombies and murdering her husband and their creator.

The war saw more zombie movies, as if the willing massacre of tens of millions of men by one another made people want to believe that all human beings were powerless killers without responsibility, particularly if they were following the orders of a maniac like Adolf Hitler. *The Voodoo Man* of 1944 showed another doctor with a zombie wife, trying to un-zombie her through other girls, whom he turned into zombies until he was shot and they were released. If it was a bad film, *Voodoo Woman* of 1956 was worse, with a mad scientist trying to turn women into the obedient slaves of male fantasy and making monsters out them. *Zombies on Broadway*, however, brought Lugosi back rather sadly, to play the role of a doctor in the West Indies who produced zombies by injection. He would have done better to have left the living dead and himself out of the picture.

If bad movies ended the zombie movie, it was not from want of trying to exploit the name. The last of the forties movies, *Valley of the Zombies,* had nothing to do with zombies at all. It featured the usual insane scientist who returned from the dead and prolonged his life by stealing blood from a doctor. A mere bullet, though, killed him in the end. Luckily, this inanity went out on a double bill with the interesting *The Catman of Paris,* which had all the charm of a Feuillade serial like *Fantomas.*

Later zombies were mere exploitation words in the title of films. *Teenage Zombies* of 1957 exploited the success of *I Was a Teenage Frankenstein. Voodoo Island* of 1957 was only interesting because Boris Karloff was in it. Only *The Zombies of Mora Tau* was pretty faithful to old legend. These were the guardians of an underwater treasure; when it was destroyed, they vanished. *(See Colour Section)* To cash in on the Karloff title, the film was also called *The Dead That Walk.*

Like other movies of the undead, zombie pictures went in for more and more gore. It might have seemed impossible to surpass the horror sequences of the zom-

The zombies advance in *The Zombies of Mora-Tau,* also called *The Dead That Walk.*

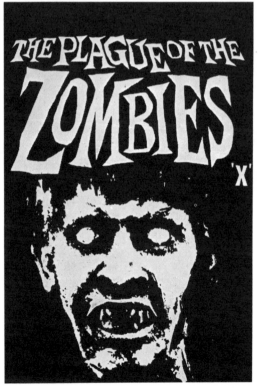

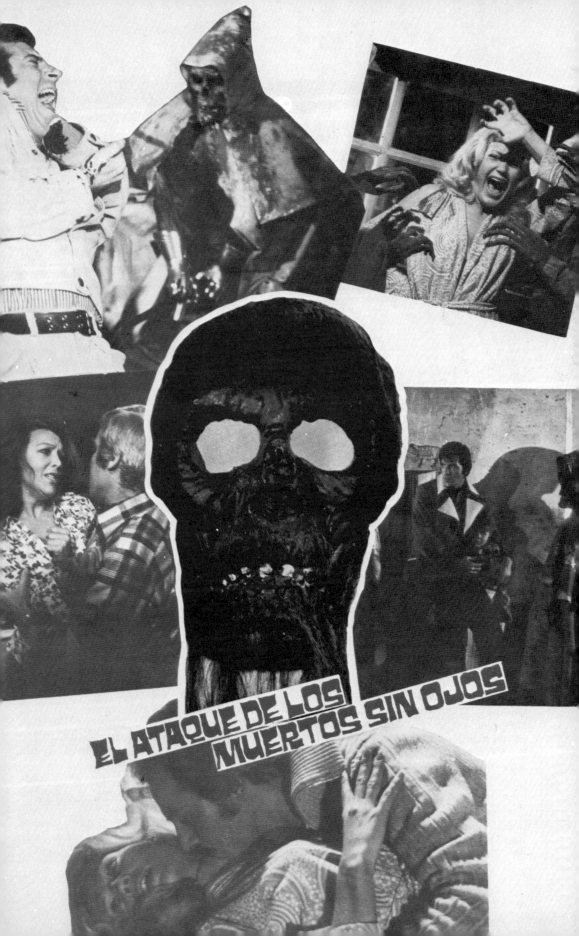

EL ATAQUE DE LOS MUERTOS SIN OJOS

bie in *The Four Skulls of Jonathan Drake*. Yet in *I Eat Your Skin*, not suprisingly billed with *I Drink Your Blood*, an adventurer battled a horde of laboratory-made zombies on an island. The gore dripped, the suspense lacked.

Otherwise, zombies were treated historically by the countries of their making. The Mexicans predictably put the pudgy wrestling superhero Santo against the undead in *Invasion of the Zombies*. The Italians constructed a zombie army of dead Roman legionaries and tribesmen to threaten the world with the rule of a black magician rather than an Emperor. The picture was variously called *Rome vs. Rome* or *War of the Zombies*. The English created a tyrannical Victorian mine-owner in Cornwall, who used zombies to work his tin as slave labour; the only merit of *Plague of the Zombies* was a dream sequence of the dead rising from their graves. And finally, the Spanish made a fearsome zombie picture from one part of their

tradition, *The attack of the Eyeless Dead* of 1972, in which a dead Military Order of Knights rose from its graves to terrorise a village.

More satisfactory than these limited attempts to use the zombie myth of the living dead controlled by *humans* was the suggestion of living corpses controlled by *aliens*. Boris Karloff playing Dr Rukh in *The Invisible Ray* of 1936 set a fashion for scientists controlled by an alien influence and causing death to all — in this case, the influence was mere radioactivity from a meteorite. More influential was Howard Hawks's film of 1951, *The Thing (From Another World)* in which the killer alien from the frozen flying saucer used human blood to fertilise its seeds.

The Thing has become the most seminal of all the pictures of alien intelligences using human blood. But the prototype of aliens using human shapes was Don Siegel's *Invasion of the Body Snatchers,* later taken to be an allegory

Above: The plant seeds of *The Thing . . .* fertilised by human blood, begin to grow. *Below:* The giant plants of *Invasion of the Body Snatchers* (1955) begin to grow . . .

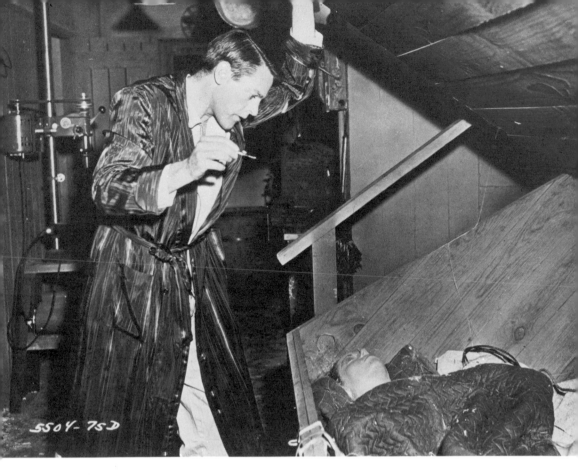

Above: And their pods turn into zombie replicas of the people of the town, controlled by alien intelligences. **Below:** The hero and heroine flee from the possessed townspeople in *Invasion of the Body Snatchers*.

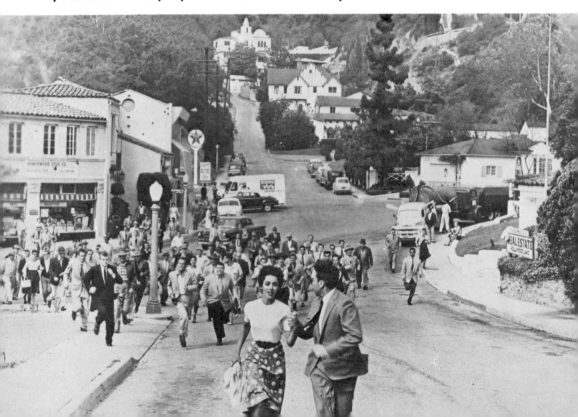

The *Invisible Invaders* advance in 1959.

about brain-washing through fluoride or McCarthyism — at the time, though, it only seemed to be a superbly crafted thriller. Alien influences grew great plants in the hothouses of a small American town. These produced large pods, which burst open to reveal the replicas of people. These replicas rose and killed their originals, and they forced the hero and heroine to flee for their lives. She also became possessed by the aliens, until only he was left to warn the passing and heedless cars on a highway that the aliens were coming.

Although none of the later alien-controlled zombie films had Siegel's touch of class, *Invisible Invaders* was interesting in its scene of the corpses walking forwards, animated by intelligences from the Moon. Only blasts of sound could destroy these risen dead. Unfortunately, its relative success led to sequels such as *The Earth Dies Screaming* of 1964 and *Night of the Living Dead* of 1968, in which radiation

The corpses from beneath the earth start their mayhem among the alive in *Night of the Living Dead* (1968).

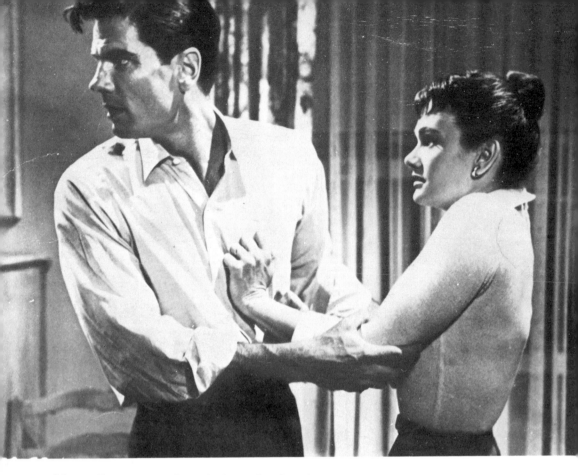

Above: A moment of marital tension in *I Married a Monster From Outer Space* (1958). *Below:* The children in *Village of the Damned* (1960) mass together in their strange communion . . .

from space caused the dead to get up and devour the living. Why this last film has become something of an underground cult remains as much of a mystery as the actual alien influence controlling the Living Dead. Ghoulish and grisly the film may be, but its wooden-looking undead made Lugosi at his most somnolent look like Nijinsky.

As a matter of reproducing themselves, aliens could choose the normal method with earth women rather than seed-pods or walking corpses. *I Married a Monster From Outer Space* was a brilliant title in itself, and a cheap way of making a movie. The aliens in the case had decided to make themselves into replicas of married men in order to replenish their dying

And some of them come closer to work their will on us.

species. More interesting was *Villiage of the Damned,* in which the women of an English village fell asleep for twenty-four hours and woke to find themselves all pregnant. Their children were mysterious, telepathetic, bonded together in a secret, capable of influencing others to perform their mass will. Such an event had happened once before in village history, and all the children had been killed for it. This time we are left with the dilemma — if they survive, will we not be taken over by a group with alien fathers?

There were other more conventional

The blank stare denotes alien possession in *Not of this Earth* (1956).

The skull to be animated is kept in a safe in *Not of This Earth*.

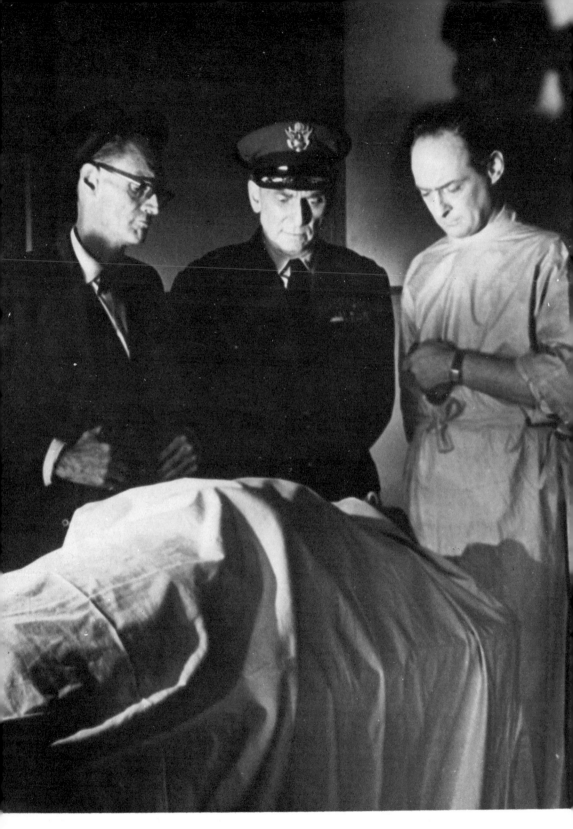

The military are worried at a victim of the *Fiend Without a Face* (1958), because he has had his head emptied like an egg.

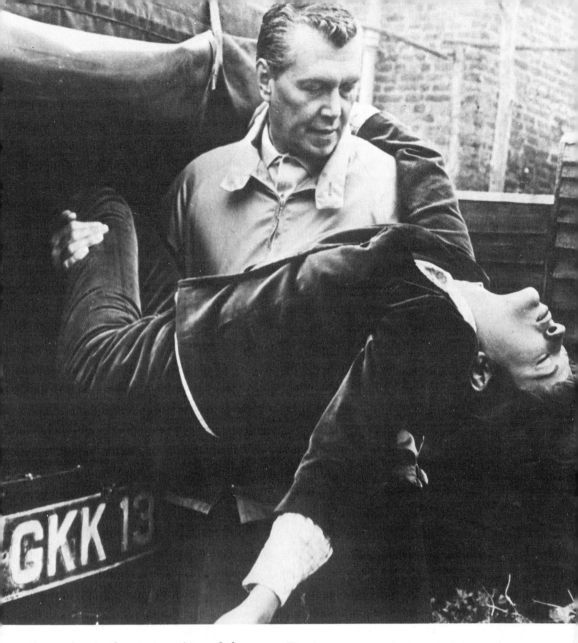

films about the possession of human shapes by alien intelligences. The glazed stare of the blood-drinking man possessed by an alien in *Not of This Earth* did suggest other worldly control, even if the idea of the skull kept in the safe seemed more Frankenstein than Further Space. Also gory was *Fiend Without a Face,* in which alien thoughts actually became matter. Crawling and flying brains whizzed about and sucked human brains from their skulls. It was enough to make a thinking man leave the cinema before it was too late.

Rather absurd also was *They Came*

The hero saves the heroine from the alien intelligence in human corpses in *They Came From Beyond Space* (1967).

From Beyond Sapce, in which alien intelligences arrived on meteorites, took over dead bodies and spread the plague. When the hero and heroine got back to the Moon to see why the aliens had invaded, they found that the aliens needed slaves to repair their wrecked space-ship. Still, the idea of extra-terrestial intelligences taking over our bodies and souls has a long history. People often call it religion.

THE FUTURE OF THE BURIED

So the zombie walks among us in many disguises, and he represents many of our fears. In only two things is he always the same. He is the dead-and-alive, the walking corpse. And he follows the will of another, for he had none of his own.

First of all, he represents our ancient fear that a necromancer will resurrect our body for his purposes. If the necromancer is now played by a mad scientist, it is still the old myth in modern dress. In *The Mad Ghoul*, for instance, David Bruce played the dead-and-alive zombie, his walking trance induced by George Zucco's special gas.

To stay semi-alive, he had to kill people and rob graves, because he kept on needing a supply of fresh human hearts — an early case of surgical transplants.

Another ancient fear is that we may be preserved dead-and-alive for ever, as if we were waxworks of ourselves. There have been films patterned on the original *Waxworks* and *The Mystery of the Wax Musuem*, in which the disfigured sculptor Lionel Atwill hid his frightful face under a wax mask and put his murder victims

The masked George Zucco examines his zombie in *The Mad Ghouls* (1943).

David Bruce is stricken by the body he has killed in *The Mad Ghoul*.

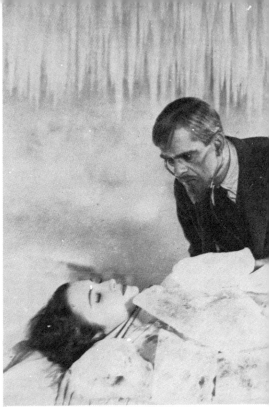

Above left: Lionel Attwill makes a nude sculpture before he is disfigured in *The Mystery of the Wax Museum* (1932). *Above right:* Jo Ann Sayers is put on ice by Boris Karloff in *The Man With Nine Lives* (1940). *Below:* Vincent Price steals a body from the morgue to use as the basis for a wax sculpture in *House of Wax* (1953).

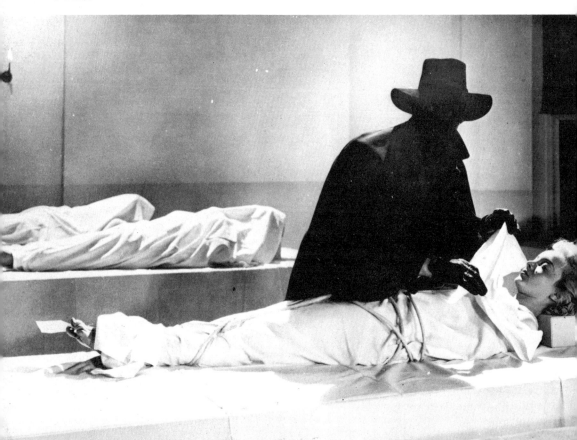

The dead are refrigerated until they are needed for experiments in *The Frozen Dead* (1966), starring Dana Andrews.

inside statues of wax, because he could no longer sculpt them. These films play on the fear that our bodies may be used as models or for necrophilia by evil people. The trouble is that, like Galatea, we may be made to rise again as zombies, breaking through the wax mask that encases us — or the ice.

For that ancient legend of men buried in ice and being woken up after the centuries of suspended animation has become modern burial practice. When Boris Karloff played *The Man With Nine Lives* in 1940, his part of Dr Kravaal believed that he could cure cancer by freezing people. Unfortunately, he and the suspicious police were all frozen solid in his underground ice chamber in a near-

by glacier. Ten years later, he was revived to find that freezing did cure cancer, only the formula was lost. The trouble was that reality, as usual, has caught up with the science fiction of the cinema, and people are already having their bodies frozen after death — to be revived at a later date when their diseases or old age become curable. In *The Frozen Dead*, the corpses of the Nazi soldiers hang in the ice-chamber like sides of beef, and even the hoary old talking head is animated by electric wiring. Only unfortunately, in the age of refrigeration and transplants, this

The severed head talks in *The Frozen Dead*.

seems all too near to us.

Another fear of the undead lies in our unquiet conscience, that a wronged person will return from the grave to avenge himself. The theme of Poe's 'House of Usher' or 'Ligeia' is really the theme of the ravages of love or conscience conjuring up the implacable dead.

Of course, this theme can be used as disguise in a murder mystery, where the murderer pretends to be buried and returns from the dead with a perfect alias, as in *The Curse of the Living Corpse*.

The vampire is, naturally, the most disturbing of our fears, because of our superstitions about human blood and our need for it after bad accidents. In the depths of the night, the vampire comes upon us — particularly upon women. There is certainly a connection between the menstruation of women and their fear of the vampire — blood is deep in the body and the psyche. Thus the emergence and dominance of the lady vampires in recent continental and British horror films is based on the physiology of women, needing to renew their blood with their fertility, as well as on ancient Balkan superstitions.

Above: The resurrected Madeline takes her vengeance in Corman's *The Fall of the House of Usher. Below:* Vincent Price battles for his life against his resurrected first wife in Corman's *Tomb of Ligeia.*

Above: The murderer is officially buried in *The Curse of the Living Corpse* (1963) . . .
Below: Then he returns from the dead to threaten the maiden.

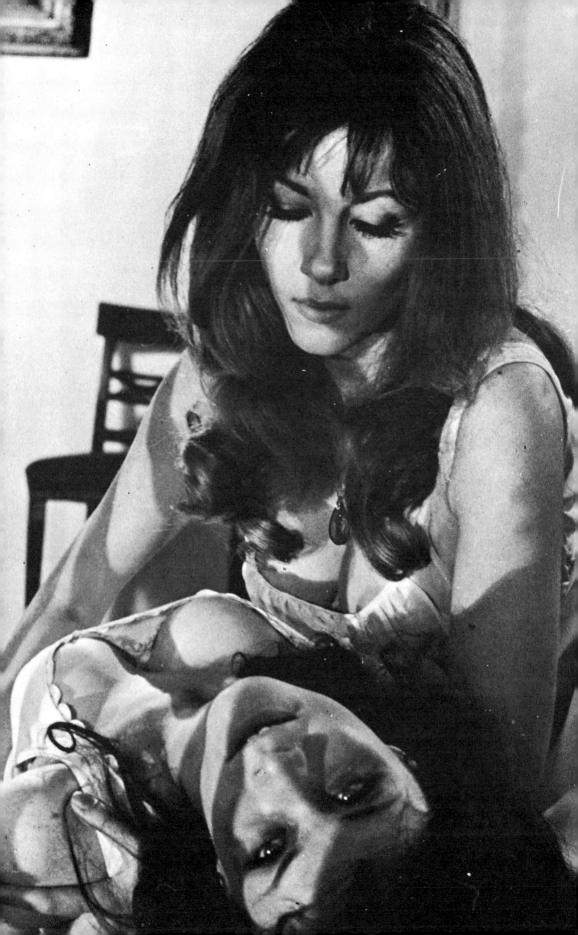

Ingrid Pitt bending over her victim-to-be leads a host of vampire ladies from Hammer Films . *Above:* Hammer again . *Below:* . . . and Continental Variations.

Karloff as The Mummy.

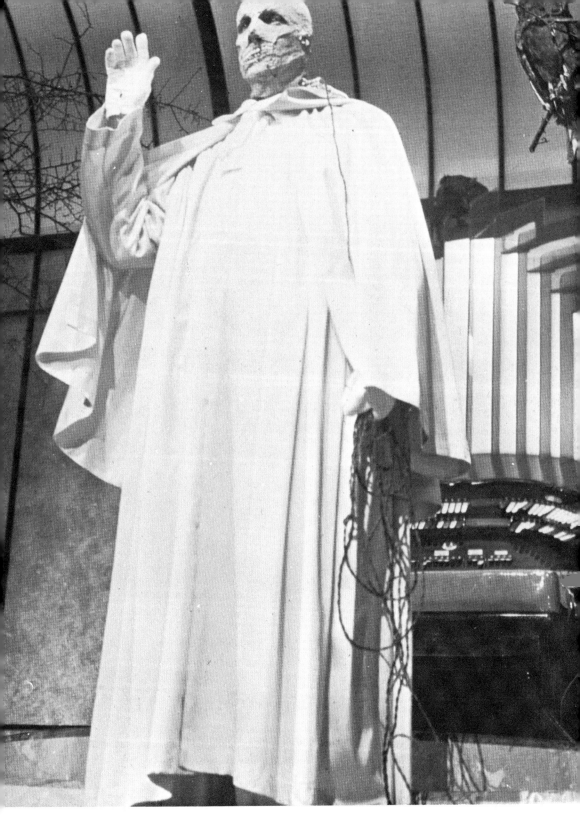

In *The Abominable Dr Phibes* (1971), Vincent Price plays the risen dead for laughs as well as horror.

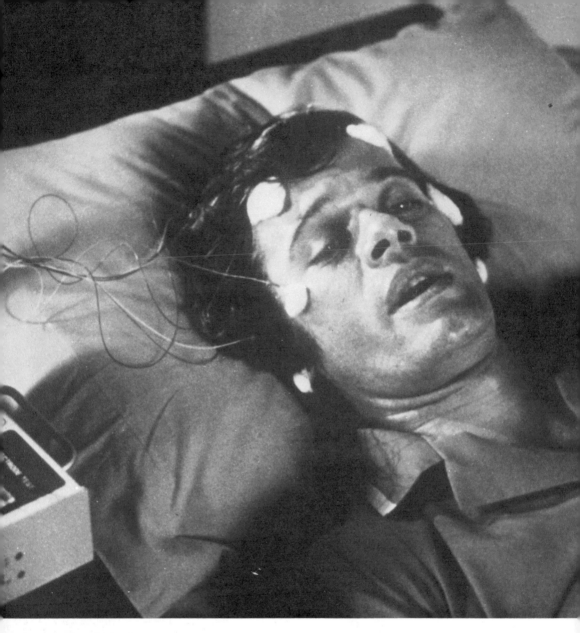

Michael Sarrazin tries to find his dead self in *The Resurrection of Peter Proud* (1974).

Yet the Mummy was where it all began. There the dead were wrapped up, waiting only to be disturbed in order to rise again. The cult of the reincarnation of the dead grew and became part of us all. And even though it can be masked and made camp, it still represents a secret inward longing and fear, that one day there will be a resurrection, that one day there may be a new life.

We are certainly part of the great chain of the living and the dead. It is even possible that we have been born before, as was the obsession of Peter Proud. And we often feel that we are controlled by forces greater than ourselves — invisible invaders that make us do their will. It is impossible to walk through life without occasionally thinking that we are zombies of necessity and fate. We exist but a space. When we die, we hope to rest in peace. But will we? Can we be sure that our body will stay still after death? Or will it go on working for the will of another?

The body seems dematerialized in George Segal's recent remake of *The Maltese Falcon,* now called *The Black Bird.*